Corporate World Meets Jesus

Growing Your Business with Christ in the Center

Dr. Christine Rice Slocumb

Copyright © 2017 Dr. Christine Rice Slocumb

All rights reserved. No part of this book may be reproduced or transmitted in any form or by any means for commercial gain or profit without written permission of the author. Scripture is taken from the New King James Version New Spirit-Filled Life Bible© 2002 by Thomas Nelson, Inc. Other references: Message Bible

This publication is sold with the understanding that neither the publisher nor the author shall be held liable for any damages. Special thanks to the Unsplash.com and Pixybay.com artist for allowing the use of artwork and photography.

Published by Dr. Christine Rice Slocumb

Emerald Coast Florida

For more information, please contact: 478-714-8262

Internet: www.drchristinericeslocumb.com

All rights reserved

ISBN-13: 978-1723484087

From The Author

Hi, thank you so much for blessing me by purchasing your book. This short but yet authoritative text is created to give you a brief overview of what it would look like to bring Jesus into your world of business.

Please know that you have sown seed on good ground. I pray that you will be uplifted and encouraged by the words you read. I pray that "the God of our Lord Jesus Christ, the Father of glory, give to you the spirit of wisdom and revelation in the knowledge of Him." (Ephesians 1:17)

It is always a pleasure to share with others what Father God gives to me. As you continue on life's journey, may you be true to yourself, be that person God created you to be, regardless of what others may think.

I command in the name of Jesus the Christ of Nazareth that all the gifts and talents that Father God has put in you if not activated be activated now! So that you can share with the world through your business the vision and the message He has given to you to make a difference in the life of everyone you serve and to build up the Kingdom of God.

Many blessings to you! And may you have an awesome forever. *Dr. Christine Rice Slocumb*

Dr. Christine Rice Slocumb

For workshops and or speaking engagements inbox
drchristinericeslocumb@gmail.com

INTRODUCTION

I have a confession to make. I know if you are reading this book you are probably saying WHAT???? Confession???? Yep, so here it goes.
When this book was put in my spirit to write, the title started out as "Spirituality in the Market Place," then it changed to "Corporate World Meets Spirituality."

I even email a close friend of mine to get her opinion on the title. I toiled back and forth like a ship tossing and turning in the ocean riding out massive waves. So, after all, was said and done, guess who had the final word? Yep, certainly from the title, you guessed it. Jesus!!

You see, spirituality represents mystical, unworldly, otherworldly, psychic, nonphysical, and transcendent. Wikipedia defines spirituality as referring to almost any kind of meaningful activity, especially a "search for the sacred." It may also refer to personal growth, blissful experience, or an encounter with one's own "inner dimension." That's okay, but holds no real life-changing power that lasts for an eternity.

Father God brought to my memory the problem with society today is that Jesus is not represented in the lives of most people as He should be. Therefore the world is in chaos; just the mention of His name is offensive to some.

Think about it for a second. The name of Jesus is the only name that humanity is restricted to say in the cooperate world. Christians, Jews, and the Christianity faith and Judaism seem to always be under attack. The principles of the different faith traditions of

Catholic, Hindus, Buddhists, and secularists (atheists and agnostics) and every other religion and name can be worshiped and talked about, 'but no not' Jesus.
It is a proven fact that Christianity, God's Word, Jesus the Father, Son and the Holy Spirit saves, heals and delivers people from bondage, yes the whole man spirit, body, and soul. Society has been trying for decades to squash the name of Jesus, and I can assure you it will never happen.

    The name of Jesus has so much power, and it's in Him alone that human beings individually, or collectively are saved. It is in Him we live move and have our nature, so to implement an environment without Jesus is not a wise choice. Therefore, the title of this book became "Corporate World Meets JESUS" to encourage you to allow Christ to be the center of not only your life but your business.

    Let's take a look at some of the marketplaces which allow Jesus to be a part of their company, to name a few that you may be familiar. Mind you, not only big corporations, small individual Entrepreneurship as well.

Cynthia's Hair and Nails: I have the pleasure of going there on a regular basis. Her beauty salon is like no other. Not only do men and women get their hair done but Christian music and videos play all day, there is no gossip. Customers who want to can receive prayer. Each person is treated special and leaves full-field.

Forever 21: Printed on the bottom of their store bags are biblical references.

Tyson Foods: They embrace spirituality in the

workplace. Tyson foods employ chaplains (compassionate pastoral care.)

Chick-Fil-A Everyone knows it is a Christian business. They demonstrate it within their establishment and the employees they hire. God blesses the industry. Have you ever seen an empty parking lot at Chick-Fil-A, other than on Sundays which is set aside to observe the Sabbath?

Mary Kay: Owner elected to take God as her partner.

In & Out Burger: Bible verses printed on the company's material.

Timberland: Jewish Faith. Owner believes you shall treat the stranger with dignity.

Alaska Air: Gives out bible note cards to customers from the Old Testament.

Hobby Lobby: Their mission statement is "Honoring the Lord in all we do by operating the company in a manner consistent with biblical principles."

Service Master: Their foundational commitment is "To honor God in all we do."

H.E.B. Grocery Store Chain: The owner is a religious reformer who connected with Billy Graham in the 1950's.

    Those are just a few companies that I found through my research. At the end of the book are additional resources of other Faith Base companies.

These businesses are not only prospering but making a difference in the lives of those they serve and those that labor among them. So why not invite Jesus into your corporation? You have nothing to lose, but everything to gain. Let's face it, who does the work? And how do you the employer engage with the employees you hire?

"Find someone that has a passion for their job, and the work that they do, then equip them to do it, and you will have a trusted, happy, productive employee for life." – Dr. Christine Rice Slocumb

"A Strong Business Mindset Includes The Things Of God." – Dr. Christine Rice Slocumb

Dr. Christine Rice Slocumb

CONTENTS

From The Author

1. Not Ashamed Of The Gospel — 15
2. Inequality? Not Me! — 21
3. Vision — 38
4. Strategic Planning — 40
5. Customer Service — 44
6. Success — 48
7. Resources — 62

Place Your Life before God
Romans 12: 1-2 (Message Bible Translation)

So here's what I want you to do, God helping you: Take your everyday, ordinary life – your sleeping, eating, going-to-work, and walking –around life and place it before God as an offering.

Embracing what God does for you is the best thing you can do for Him.

Don't become so well –adjusted to your culture that you fit into it without even thinking. Instead, fix your attention on God. You'll be changed from the inside out.

Readily recognize what He wants from you, and quickly respond to it. Unlike the culture around you, always dragging you down to its level of immaturity, God brings the best out of you, develops well-formed maturity in you.

Corporate World Meets Jesus

Growing Your Business with Christ in the Center

Dr. Christine Rice Slocumb

Dr. Christine Rice Slocumb

CHAPTER 1

NOT ASHAMED OF THE GOSPEL

"A company that prays together grows together."
– Dr. Christine Rice Slocumb

Healthy corporations grow faster than weak ones, Right??? Umm Yeah!! But the reality is, how often do you earnestly think about keeping it healthy?

"Unity within the workforce can be one way to prevent high turnover." –Dr. Christine Rice Slocumb

If you have influential senior leaders that understand the company's vision and where it is going, then they can relate it to co-workers so that they feel connected to the company's idea as well. Too often there is no communication between the senior leaders and co-workers which eventually creates office hostility.

Heck, some employees never see the director or much less the supervisor. Yep! I know to be the person in charge you may not have time for the lower class as some would say. Helloooo! Can I introduce you to a man who is the King of Kings and Lord of lords who has time for people from all walks of life? His name is Jesus. If you elect, to allow Him, to be a part of your business, you will have to engage with your employees at some point.

"When the CEO of a company has the heart to see and sit with those who labor among them, they gain respect." –Dr. Christine Rice Slocumb

Reasons People Leave a Job

There are many justifications for why people leave jobs, granted not all motives are wrong. For the most part, people move from a position because of employee dissatisfaction, hostile work environments, and high expectations of rapid reproductions. Boredom, and no room for growth, overworked and underpaid which leads to levels of stress. Inadequate resources to do the job due to financial cutbacks. No Attaboy from the employer, meaning, co-workers feel that their effort does not make a difference and therefore a commitment to and the quality of their work is compromised. Situations where co-workers cannot get along which creates a hostile and possibly dangerous work environment.

Some familiar sources of problems and failure in a work environment is a result of mismatched personalities in positions. That said, it is wise for companies today to understand and distinguish between someone who can do a job but doesn't like it, and someone who is suitable for the job and can do it. In both cases, productivity results can be negative or positive.

Furthermore, there are situations where employees will leave a company for good reasons. Perhaps a relocation, retirement or promotion. Moreover, sad to say, but the bad seems to outweigh the good regarding leaving the workplace.

Reasons People Stay At A Job.

Just as there are reasons people leave a job, there are reasons people chose to stay. To name a few. Comfortable salary, pension, benefits and additional perks. A source of freedom to the job, meaning no micromanager. The company promotes from within when new positions become available. Raises are lovely, and employees feel that they are a part of a team. Work atmosphere is thriving and productive.

Some people may not like the job, but stay because they need to work and support a family. They have bills to pay and fear that if they left to pursue what their heart truly desires, they might not be successful. So they stay in the position because of the provision. In my opinion, the need for money to survive from day to day describes the majority of people in the world.

"People have a desire to be wanted, needed and accomplished. If a corporation can tap into the heart's core desire of their employees and keep Jesus in the center of it all the results would deliver an unshakable partnership combination." – Dr. Christine Rice Slocumb

True story I was hired to work for this company let's call it division" because that is what happens within this organization. Upon hire, my position was to manage the high-risk cases that each case manager handled assuring that the treatment plans for the clients were on task. Following that, I was to examine case managers monthly case reviews to make sure they were on the right track. My position also included to facilitate support groups and come up with training exercises for the case managers. Now, first of all. If case managers themselves are not healed and free from bondage, meaning they have pressing issues to deal with in their own life. Most likely they will not be able to meet the needs of others appropriately. Please don't misunderstand what I'm saying. I know we all have something in life we are battling, but if you cannot get free yourself and deal with your emotional pain, failures, and insecurity, you are no help to others.

    I know you have heard the saying that there is always one bad apple. And one bad apple does not spoil the show? Ha! Not an entirely accurate statement. In this story that I am sharing with you, there was one bad apple that destroyed the whole show. This apple was so bad it disrupted the flow of helping families and even influenced the people who served under it to operate in the same demonic spirit.

    This apple was so evil that just the mention of Jesus name made it angry. Upon entering a workplace, most people greet each other with a good morning and a smile, common courtesies, right? Wrong. The co-workers in this office told me, and I quote, "I pissed in their morning." seriously? By just a simple smile and a hello. Wow!

    This apple was so bad that the Regional Director was afraid to confront the lousy apple about their behavior. This apple was so bad that it ignored everything it was supposed to do in my presence. Mind you; I was the supervisor.

    Communicating with this individual was impossible. The employees in this office made fun and talked about the families we served in such a wrong way; I was in shock! I thought Wow! What if this was your family? One of the office administrators said the baby of the family we were serving looked like a chimpanzee. Upon that statement made, the other case managers laughed. The sad part of that is the office employee who made that statement failed to recognize that she was pregnant, and her baby was yet to be born. (Be careful what you say and how you treat others, we reap what we sow.) Her baby once she gave birth, died of crib death. 'Just saying.'

The work atmosphere and this place of employment was an open office; the only privacy was a partition. Therefore ever conversation was heard, even the case managers personal issues. Because of that environment and the unwillingness of the director to handle the situation, I was the third person to resign from that department. I learned that several others in the past who worked there quit, by walking off the job with no notice. Long story short, after my resignation the Regional Director, was terminated.

Now let's look at several things that were operating in this environment.

1. Communication was weak between the director/supervisor and employees.

2. The Love of God was not welcome in that place.

3. Employees talked horribly about their clients and made fun of the client's situations.

4. No respect for co-workers individually and or workspace.

5. Jealously and envy played a significant role.

6. Heavy caseloads, low morale and low pay.

7. Personal issues which flowed over into the work environment.

    There is so much I could add to this list, but you get my drift, right? So, with that said the office had no direction, vision or oneness and defiantly no real productivity. Being the third person who resigned from that office, management never responded to my letter or reach out to understand the reason why I left. Today that office still has turmoil and families are not getting the proper intervention needed to enhance their lives.
    I shared this brief story because had Christ been represented, and there were grief support services for the employees, the atmosphere in that office would have been conducive to a spirit of love and understanding. Working in unity would have been demonstrated for the betterment of the families who needed our service.

CHAPTER 2

INEQUALITY? NOT ME

You have a business. Great! Let me ask you a question. Are you fair and just in your dealings? Do you have an issue hiring someone because of the color of their skin, handicap or gender? Do you offer equal pay among your employees? Do you show favoritism among your employees? Don't get offended and stop reading; I'm just asking a few simple questions. If by chance any of these questions put a ruffle in your feather, you may want to consider doing a heart check, why? Because something within the heart is in need of healing and only Jesus can heal the heart of humanity. You see, it's like this, you cannot grow your business in Christ with any inequality in your heart. Sure, your company is flourishing and may continue for a season, but at some point there will come some form of distress along the way which can only be resolved with the help of the Lord.

Wikipedia defines occupational inequality as "The unequal treatment of people based on gender, sexuality, height, weight, accent, or race in the workplace. When researchers study trends in occupational inequality they usually focus on distribution or allocation pattern of groups across occupations, for example, the distribution of men compared to women in a certain occupation. Secondly, they focus on the link between occupation and income, for example, comparing the income of whites with blacks in the same occupation."
The UK Government puts discrimination into the following four categories:

Direct discrimination: Treating someone different than others (like paying someone less money than others because of who they are).

Indirect discrimination: Putting rules in place that apply to everyone, but puts someone else at an unfair disadvantage (like having job requirements that exclude disabled people).

Harassment: Unwanted behavior linked to someone's differences such as name-calling, bullying and stereotyping.

Victimization: Mistreating someone because they've complained about discrimination or harassment.

Equality means making sure people are given equal opportunities, equal pay and are accepted for their differences. It is disheartening to see that in 2018 inequality exist on such a massive level.
One significant difference today is that instead of hiding faces with hoods, discrimination is now masked in a suit and tie attire and sitting behind a desk. It is in the grocery store, restaurant, driving and walking on the streets, and worse, in the church as people sit in pews every Sunday.

It is true that from the beginning of time inequality existed then and it is apparent it will continue until Jesus returns. It wasn't right then and it's not right today. The cool thing is we have the power to change it one person at a time, one business at a time, one law at a time, and ultimately with prayer. Pray does change things. You may be asking yourself this question; "Am I the type of owner who has treated others unfair? Well if that answer is yes, you can repent and ask Father God to forgive you.

Go back to those areas or persons if you can, and asked for forgiveness' and make it right. Change rules if they need to be changed and apologize to those you have wronged. You will feel better and so will your company, and those you have mistreated.

"Forgiveness sets you free and opens the door to greatness." Dr. Christine Rice Slocumb

I have experienced levels of inequality within the marketplace. While looking for employment, I received calls from different companies wanting to hire. When I would show up, suddenly they would have a change of heart. I had one manager of a hospice facility, yes! Hospice, go figure, located on the emerald coast of Florida, tell me to my face that they were looking for the perfect fit. Now mind you, they called me for the interview. I was totally qualified for the position. I had the interview with the assistant manager first. She was overjoyed and told me that the manager would be happy to have someone with my credentials and attitude.

The assistant manager arranged a second interview to meet the manager. As I walked into the managers office and took a seat, she took one look at me, and at that moment in her discriminate mind, announced to me that I was not the perfect fit, that they were looking for the perfect fit! I asked her what the perfect fit was. As we dialogued back and forth, she could not tell me; she just exclaimed repeatedly, "oh! Just the perfect fit." Really??? I thought in my mind, "Did she say that to me? And handle me this way?" After the interview, the assistant manager contacted me and apologized for the behavior of the manager.

My Lord, But God, that I have the heart of Jesus because it could have been a shocking day for the manager, meaning; I really could have, and probably should have filed a discrimination case against her and the company. Instead, I let Father God fight that battle. However, I did communicate to the manager that she had the perfect fit sitting in front of her and that she will not find anyone else for that position because she will always be looking for the perfect fit. To date, 2 years later, the same position is continuously advertised.

"Be watchful; sometimes God will send people to your organization to be a blessing?"- Dr. Christine Rice Slocumb

Something I ponder on a bit. Located on an employment application are questions that do not determine if a person can do the job or not. For instance. Race, gender, handicap, military, and age. Now upon choosing which block to check, determines how a person's application will be received. Say what you want; all of that weighs in on the hiring factor. Honestly, does any of that information let the employer know that this person can do the job? Heck no!! It's to shift people out that they feel are undesirable for the position. Yeah, I know, you are thinking- "well that is done to avoid inequality, it's good for the Census Bureau. Yeah, I know, they keep official count or surveys on people, places, economy and so forth. Understandable, but those records are not justifiable.

"Who knows better what inequality is; except for the one who discrimination has taken place?"- Dr. Christine Rice Slocumb.

This information comes directly from the US Equal Employment Opportunity Commission:

Age Discrimination
Age discrimination involves treating an applicant or employee less favorably because of his or her age. The Age Discrimination in Employment Act (ADEA) forbids age discrimination against people who are age 40 or older. It does not protect workers under the age

of 40, although some states have laws that protect younger workers from age discrimination. It is not illegal for an employer or other covered entity to favor an older worker over a younger one, even if both workers are age 40 or older. Discrimination can occur when the victim and the person who inflicted the discrimination are both over 40.

Age Discrimination & Work Situations

The law prohibits discrimination in any aspect of employment, including hiring, firing, pay, job assignments, promotions, layoff, training, benefits, and any other term or condition of employment.

Age Discrimination & Harassment

It is unlawful to harass a person because of his or her age. Harassment can include, for example, offensive or derogatory remarks about a person's age. Although the law doesn't prohibit simple teasing, offhand comments, or isolated incidents that aren't very serious, harassment is illegal when it is so frequent or severe that it creates a hostile or offensive work environment or when it results in an adverse employment decision (such as the victim being fired or demoted). The harasser can be the victim's supervisor, a supervisor in another area, a co-worker, or someone who is not an employee of the employer, such as a client or customer.

Age Discrimination & Employment Policies/Practices

An employment policy or practice that applies to everyone, regardless of age, can be illegal if it has a negative impact on applicants or employees age 40 or older and is not based on a reasonable factor other than age (RFOA).

Disability Discrimination

Disability discrimination occurs when an employer or

other entity covered by the Americans with Disabilities Act, as amended, or the Rehabilitation Act, as amended, treats a qualified individual with a disability who is an employee or applicant unfavorably because she has a disability. Learn more about the Act at **ADA at 25**.

Disability discrimination also occurs when a covered employer or other entity treats an applicant or employee less favorably because she has a history of a disability. (such as cancer that is controlled or in remission) or because she is believed to have a physical or mental impairment that is not transitory (lasting or expected to last six months or less) and minor (even if she does not have such an impairment).

The law requires an employer to provide reasonable accommodation to an employee or job applicant with a disability unless doing so would cause significant difficulty or expense for the employer ("undue hardship").

The law also protects people from discrimination based on their relationship with a person with a disability (even if they do not themselves have a disability). For example, it is illegal to discriminate against an employee because her husband has a disability. Note: Federal employees and applicants are covered by the Rehabilitation Act of 1973, instead of the Americans with Disabilities Act. The protections are mostly the same.

Disability Discrimination & Work Situations

The law forbids discrimination when it comes to any aspect of employment, including hiring, firing, pay, job assignments, promotions, layoff, training, fringe benefits, and any other term or condition of employment.

Disability Discrimination & Harassment

It is illegal to harass an applicant or employee because he has a disability, had a disability in the past, or is believed to have a physical or mental impairment that is not transitory (lasting or expected to last six months or less) and minor (even if he does not have such an impairment).

Harassment can include, for example, offensive remarks about a person's disability. Although the law doesn't prohibit simple teasing, offhand comments, or isolated incidents that aren't very serious, harassment is illegal when it is so frequent or severe that it creates a hostile or offensive work environment or when it results in an adverse employment decision (such as the victim being fired or demoted).

The harasser can be the victim's supervisor, a supervisor in another area, a co-worker, or someone who is not an employee of the employer, such as a client or customer.

Disability Discrimination & Reasonable Accommodation:

The law requires an employer to provide reasonable accommodation to an employee or job applicant with a disability unless doing so would cause significant difficulty or expense for the employer. A reasonable accommodation is any change in the work environment (or in the way things are usually done) to help a person with a disability apply for a job, perform the duties of a job, or enjoy the benefits and privileges of employment.

Reasonable accommodation might include, for example, making the workplace accessible for wheelchair users or providing a reader or interpreter for someone who is blind or hearing impaired. While the federal anti-discrimination laws don't require an employer to accommodate an employee who must care for a disabled family member, the Family and Medical Leave Act (FMLA) may require an employer to take such steps. The Department of Labor enforces the FMLA. For more information, call: 1-866-487-9243.

Disability Discrimination & Reasonable Accommodation & Undue Hardship

An employer doesn't have to provide an accommodation if doing so would cause undue hardship to the employer. Undue hardship means that the accommodation would be too difficult or too expensive to provide, in light of the employer's size, financial resources, and the needs of the business. An employer may not refuse to provide an accommodation just because it involves some cost. An employer does not have to provide the exact accommodation the employee or job applicant wants. If more than one accommodation works, the employer may choose which one to provide.

Definition of Disability:

Not everyone with a medical condition is protected by the law. To be protected, a person must be qualified for the job and have a disability as defined by the law. A person can show that he or she has a disability in one of three ways:

A person may be disabled if he or she has a physical or mental condition that substantially limits a major life activity (such as walking, talking, seeing, hearing, or learning). A person may be disabled if he or she has a history of a disability (such as cancer that is in remission). A person may be disabled if he is believed to have a physical or mental impairment that is not transitory (lasting or expected to last six months or less) and minor (even if he does not have such an impairment). **Disability & Medical Exams During Employment Application & Interview Stage:** The law places strict limits on employers when it comes to asking job applicants to answer medical questions, take a medical exam, or identify a disability.

For example, an employer may not ask a job applicant to answer medical questions or take a medical exam before extending a job offer. An employer also may not ask job applicants if they have a disability (or about the nature of an obvious disability). An employer may ask job applicants whether they can perform the job and how they would perform the job, with or without reasonable accommodation. **Disability & Medical Exams After A Job Offer For Employment**

After a job is offered to an applicant, the law allows an employer to condition the job offer on the applicant answering certain medical questions or successfully passing a medical exam, but only if all new employees in the same type of job have to answer the questions or take the exam.

Disability & Medical Exams For Persons Who Have Started Working As Employees: Once a person is hired and has started work, an employer generally can only ask medical questions or require a medical exam if the employer needs medical documentation to support an employee's request for an accommodation, or if the employer believes that an employee is not able to perform a job successfully or safely because of a medical condition.

The law also requires that employers keep all medical records and information confidential and in separate medical files.

Equal Pay/Compensation Discrimination

The Equal Pay Act requires that men and women in the same workplace be given equal pay for equal work. The jobs need not be identical, but they must be substantially equal. Job content (not job titles) determines whether jobs are substantially equal. All forms of pay are covered by this law, including salary, overtime pay, bonuses, stock options, profit sharing and bonus plans, life insurance, vacation and holiday pay, cleaning or gasoline allowances, hotel accommodations, reimbursement for travel expenses, and benefits. If there is an inequality in wages between men and women, employers may not reduce the wages of either sex to equalize their pay.

An individual alleging a violation of the EPA may go directly to court and is not required to file an EEOC charge beforehand. The time limit for filing an EPA charge with the EEOC and the time limit for going to court are the same: within two years of the alleged unlawful compensation practice or, in the case of a willful violation, within three years. The filing of an EEOC charge under the EPA does not extend the time frame for going to court.

Equal Pay/Compensation and Sex Discrimination
Title VII also makes it illegal to discriminate based on sex in pay and benefits. Therefore, someone who has an Equal Pay Act claim may also have a claim under Title VII. Race/Color Discrimination: Race discrimination involves treating someone (an applicant or employee) unfavorably because he/she is of a certain race or because of personal characteristics associated with race (such as hair texture, skin color, or certain facial features). Color discrimination involves treating someone unfavorably because of skin color complexion. Race/color discrimination also can

involve treating someone unfavorably because the person is married to (or associated with) a person of a certain race or color.

Discrimination can occur when the victim and the person who inflicted the discrimination are the same race or color. Race/Color Discrimination & Work Situations The law forbids discrimination when it comes to any aspect of employment, including hiring, firing, pay, job assignments, promotions, layoff, training, fringe benefits, and any other term or condition of employment. Race/Color Discrimination & Harassment. It is unlawful to harass a person because of that person's race or color. Harassment can include, for example, racial slurs, offensive or derogatory remarks about a person's race or color, or the display of racially-offensive symbols.

Although the law doesn't prohibit simple teasing, offhand comments, or isolated incidents that are not very serious, harassment is illegal when it is so frequent or severe that it creates a hostile or offensive work environment or when it results in an adverse employment decision (such as the victim being fired or demoted). The harasser can be the victim's supervisor, a supervisor in another area, a co-worker, or someone who is not an employee of the employer, such as a client or customer.

Race/Color Discrimination & Employment Policies/Practices

An employment policy or practice that applies to everyone, regardless of race or color, can be illegal if it has a negative impact on the employment of people of a particular race or color and is not job-related and necessary to the operation of the business. For example, a "no-beard" employment policy that applies to all workers without regard to race may still be unlawful if it is not job-related and has a negative impact on the employment of African-American men (who have a predisposition to a skin condition that causes severe shaving bumps).

Religious Discrimination: Religious discrimination involves treating a person (an applicant or employee) unfavorably because of his or her religious beliefs. The law protects not only people who belong to traditional, organized religions, such as Buddhism, Christianity, Hinduism, Islam, and Judaism but also others who have sincerely held religious, ethical or moral beliefs. Religious discrimination can also involve treating someone differently because that person is married to (or associated with) an individual of a particular religion. **Religious Discrimination & Work Situations.** The law forbids discrimination when it comes to any aspect of employment, including hiring, firing, pay, job assignments, promotions, layoff, training, fringe benefits, and any other term or condition of employment. **Religious Discrimination & Harassment** It is illegal to harass a person because of his or her religion. Harassment can include, for example, offensive remarks about a person's religious beliefs or practices. Although the law doesn't prohibit simple teasing, offhand comments, or isolated incidents that aren't very serious, harassment is illegal when it is so frequent or severe that it creates a hostile or offensive work environment or when it results in an adverse employment decision (such as the victim being fired or demoted). The harasser can be the victim's supervisor, a supervisor in another area, a co-worker, or someone who is not an employee of the employer, such as a client or customer.

Religious Discrimination and Segregation
Title VII also prohibits workplace or job segregation based on religion (including religious garb and grooming practices), such as assigning an employee to a non-customer contact position because of actual or feared customer preference.

Religious Discrimination & Reasonable Accommodation

The law requires an employer or other covered entity to reasonably accommodate an employee's religious beliefs or practices unless doing so would cause more than a minimal burden on the operations of the employer's business. This means an employer may be required to make reasonable adjustments to the work environment that will allow an employee to practice his or her religion. Examples of some common religious accommodations include flexible scheduling, voluntary shift substitutions or swaps, job reassignments, and modifications to workplace policies or practices. ## Religious Accommodation/Dress & Grooming Policies
Unless it would be an undue hardship on the employer's operation of its business, an employer must reasonably accommodate an employee's religious beliefs or practices. This applies not only to schedule changes or leave for religious observances but also to such things as dress or grooming practices that an employee has for religious reasons. These might include, for example, wearing particular head coverings or other religious dress (such as a Jewish yarmulke or a Muslim headscarf), or wearing certain hairstyles or facial hair (such as Rastafarian dreadlocks or Sikh uncut hair and beard). It also includes an employee's observance of a religious

prohibition against wearing certain garments (such as pants or miniskirts).

When an employee or applicant needs a dress or grooming accommodation for religious reasons, he should notify the employer that he needs such an accommodation for religious reasons. If the employer reasonably needs more information, the employer and the employee should engage in an interactive process to discuss the request. If it would not pose an undue hardship, the employer must grant the accommodation. Religious Discrimination & Reasonable Accommodation & Undue Hardship

An employer does not have to accommodate an employee's religious beliefs or practices if doing so would cause undue hardship to the employer. An accommodation may cause undue hardship if it is costly, compromises workplace safety, decreases workplace efficiency, infringes on the rights of other employees, or requires other employees to do more than their share of potentially hazardous or burdensome work. Religious Discrimination and Employment Policies/Practices

An employee cannot be forced to participate (or not participate) in a religious activity as a condition of employment.

Sex-Based Discrimination: Sex discrimination involves treating someone (an applicant or employee) unfavorably because of that person's sex. Discrimination against an individual because of gender identity, including transgender status, or because of sexual orientation is discrimination because of sex in violation of Title VII. For more information about LGBT-related sex discrimination claims, for more information see http://www.eeoc.gov/eeoc/newsroom/wysk/enforcement_protections_lgbt_workers.cfm.

Sex Discrimination & Work Situations: The law forbids discrimination when it comes to any aspect of employment, including hiring, firing, pay, job assignments, promotions, layoff, training, fringe benefits, and any other term or condition of employment. **Sex Discrimination Harassment**
It is unlawful to harass a person because of that person's sex. Harassment can include "sexual harassment" or unwelcome sexual advances, requests for sexual favors, and other verbal or physical harassment of a sexual nature.

Harassment does not have to be of a sexual nature, however, and can include offensive remarks about a person's sex. For example, it is illegal to harass a woman by making offensive comments about women in general.

Both victim and the harasser can be either a woman or a man, and the victim and harasser can be the same sex. Although the law doesn't prohibit simple teasing, offhand comments, or isolated incidents that are not very serious, harassment is illegal when it is so frequent or severe that it creates a hostile or offensive work environment or when it results in an adverse employment decision (such as the victim being fired or demoted). The harasser can be the victim's supervisor, a supervisor in another area, a co-worker, or someone who is not an employee of the employer, such as a client or customer.

Sex Discrimination & Employment Policies/Practices
An employment policy or practice that applies to everyone, regardless of sex, can be illegal if it has a

negative impact on the employment of people of a certain sex and is not job-related or necessary to the operation of the business.

Surely as an entrepreneur, you know what the law says about inequality. What I have provided for you was something to refresh your memory and to encourage you to make sure your managers/supervisors and employees are exercising fairness in the workplace.

CHAPTER 3

VISION

Without Vision, People Perish- (Proverbs 29:18)

This Proverbs Revelation and the principle meaning behind it is that apart from God's word, society quickly spins into moral chaos. The proverbs mention above is not a stated mission, but a vision to incorporate God's guidance in all things. I am a firm believer that there will always be something lacking in business if one does not seek God's advice, wisdom, and His vision. You have a concept which turned into a visualization, and that was the purpose and plan given to you by the almighty God.

Perhaps you may be a part of someone else's idea or view, whatever the case may be, God's word says:

For I know, the plans I have for you declares the Lord, plans to prosper you and not to harm you, plans to give you hope and a future. (Jeremiah 29:11)

To take the first step in growing your business cultivate and share the vision with the county, community staff, and others. That is why the city you live in will ask you to bring a set of blueprints or plans. *"And the Lord answered me, and said, write the vision, and make it plain upon tablets, that he may run that readeth it." (Habakkuk 2:2)*

In light of that verse, not only do you develop an interest and excitement about what you are doing, you're able to create clear goals and action steps necessary for its success.

"A shared vision and achievement come from partnering with others. Moreover, it will shape your idea into something tangible to communicate it to your team and enhance the community around you."
– Dr. Christine Rice Slocumb

Let's take a look at David in the Bible. (II Samuel 7 and I Kings 5:2-3) The long-range plan of David was to build a temple. God did not allow David to construct it because of his associations with wars. However, when Solomon was chosen to succeed him, David handed Solomon the completed plan/vision for the temple and a list of materials on hand. The temple was complete after seven years of construction, and the long-range plan of David came into fulfillment.

CHAPTER 4

STRATEGIC PLANNING

"The only way to implement a strategy is God's way."
– Dr. Christine Rice Slocumb

We often fail to notice that Jesus spoke about the necessity of planning and strategy. A strategic plan is a plan of action designed to achieve a specific goal. The biblical approach is unique as its foundation and detail for the design comes from a Godly perspective. God being both humanity's creator and the Bible's author is positioned uniquely to address the challenges we face in our everyday life. That my friend includes your business as well; He knows you and the best plan of action for your growth personally and in the marketplace. Utilize your team to reach the objectives. Strategic planning will empower leaders to develop and keep the work environment fresh daily by revisiting and identifying the necessary steps to pitfalls before they happen. Strategic planning allows leaders to dream big. Part of a strategic plan is the focus. Let's take a look at what the Bible says about Solomon. He did not ask for great riches or fame for himself, but instead, he asked for wisdom so that he could lead God's people. Solomon demonstrates a critical aspect of leadership.

"Knowing where you want to go before asking others to follow you plays a vital role in the development of your company. Where are you going? What are you doing? " – Dr. Christine Rice Slocumb

Once your personal and organizational mission is defined, the methods become easier to clarify as well. God gives us tasks that require planning.

"Goal Setting is a robust process for thinking about the future and motivating oneself to turn the vision into reality." – Dr. Christine Rice Slocumb

Yes, looking towards the future is good. But also remember in the Bible in Matthew the six chapter verse 11 states "give us this day our daily bread." If you were to take that verse and apply it to your business that would mean the day to day business operation is essential.

"Today's goal for the company may not be the goal for tomorrow. Meaning, attune your ear to hear what God is saying about your business today, because He may want to shift it in another direction tomorrow." – Dr. Christine Rice Slocumb

Set milestones for your team to reach. Keep it simple to understand so it can be obtainable. Keep an open mind. Concentrate your efforts in the right place and motivate.

Group Education: **Leaders and visionaries often struggle to reach the task. There are times when the plan is not always smooth or precise. You can see the vision, know what you want, but the how to get there is a bit unclear. Group Education is designed to assist in creating and maintaining a plan and accomplishing it in both the professional and personal world, for the leaders as well as the employees.**

"Group education will ultimately lower stress within the workplace and increase productivity." – Dr. Christine Rice Slocumb

Team Building: As the saying goes, a leader is only as good as their team. The other part to that is, as the head goes the body follows. It is vital for every team member to see the vision, realize their role, then come together with other employees and fulfill the vision.

In a teambuilding workshop, the team will learn how to function as a unified body. How to appreciate each other's talents, gifts, desires, and passion. How to handle conflict and communicate well.

CHAPTER 5

CONFLICT WITHIN

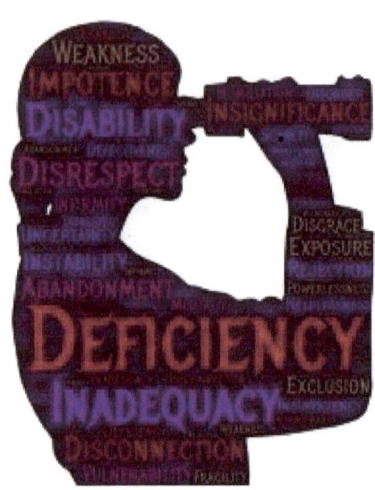 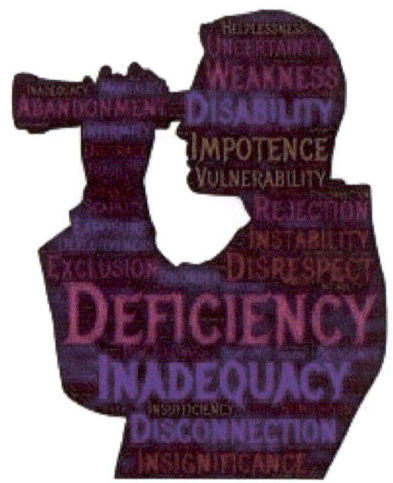

"Where do you think all these appalling wars and quarrels come from? Do you think they just happen? Think again. They come about because you want your own way, and fight for it deep inside yourselves. You lust for what you don't have and are willing to kill to get it. You want what isn't yours and will risk violence to get your hands on it. You wouldn't think of just asking God for it, would you? And why not? Because you know you'd be asking for what you have no right to. You're spoiled children, each wanting your own way. You're cheating on God. If all you want is your own way, flirting with the world every chance you get, you end up enemies of God and His way. And do you suppose God doesn't care? The proverb has it that

"He's a fiercely jealous lover." And what He gives in love is far better than anything else you'll find. It's common knowledge that God goes against the willful proud; God gives grace to the willing humble. So let God work His will in you. Yell a loud no to the devil and watch him scamper." (James 4: 1-7)

Using spiritual discernment to combat conflict within a workplace gives the opportunity for keen insight as to what is going on in the atmosphere or even individuals.

"The conflict within the workplace most often comes from the inside out of a person to include but not limited to, jealousy, anger, self-degrading, being competitive, and unhappiness with one's own life."
– Dr. Christine Rice Slocumb

The ability to discern between feelings and label them appropriately. Gaining emotional information to guide thinking and behavior will show how managing and adjusting emotions and feelings will help adapt to an environmental change and achieve one's goal.

Time Management: "Look carefully then how you walk, not as unwise but as wise, making the best use of the time because the days are evil." (Ephesians 5:15-16)

"What is time? Time is "Taking Immediate Measures Effectively for a more productive direction." – Dr. Christine Rice Slocumb

Leaders and employees should equip themselves with the necessary tools for better utilizing their time, talent, gifts and resources to accomplish goals through fresh innovated ideas. When someone is out on vacation and or has left the company, stress falls on the other team members because they now have to fill the void of doing the work required for that position until someone is hired.

Cross training will prepare your employees for the absence of a person and or position. It will minimize the cost and perhaps keep the company from losing clients or potential ones.

Employees trained in every aspect of an office function could increase the success of the company. But remember as an employer to appreciate and reward the person that has made the sacrifice to increase their workload to help the company.

"People have a desire to use their gifts, talents, experience, and passions; it's built naturally into one's DNA." – Dr. Christine Rice Slocumb

When giving the opportunity to flow freely within the workplace an individual will thrive happily and be more productive. Suddenly this employment is no longer a job to them; it becomes a part of who they are and what they were created to do.

Alignment: No one wants to be a micromanager just as no one likes to be micromanaged. Often you may find employees going in an opposite direction of the vision. Most employees want to know how aligning one with the company's vision will help them in the long run. The alignment aims to reestablish the concept, then give way for your employees to use their creative juices to accomplish the task. Some companies have surveillance and watch employees every move. Each stroke on the keyboard is monitored all day. Imagine the stress of knowing you are being watched on candid camera. Let your employees know you trust them.

"Spending time to acknowledge and develop employee's core values and their uniqueness will create a healthy atmosphere and offer great customer service that will meet the need of the clients you serve and grow your business." – Dr. Christine Rice Slocumb

"Hire people within your business who love people. If the company is people focus than hire people who have the passion for serving others" – Dr. Christine Rice Slocumb

CHAPTER 6

CUSTOMER SERVICE

    Customer service has changed tremendously. How are the customer service skills within your organization? With technology as it is you can have customers from around the globe from all walks of life. Therefore the way you offer your services is very essential. Have we all heard the saying 'the customer is always right? Wrong; sometimes, the customer is dead wrong, and it's apparent, to the point you may want to go bonkers and even make sarcastic remarks. Guess what? Giving excellent customer service requires you to take another approach.

So what should you do? Scripture tells us in (Galatians 6:1) "If a person gets trapped by doing wrong, those of you who are spiritual should help that person turn away from doing wrong. Do it gently. At the same time watch yourself so that you also are not tempted." Think about how quickly an argument can develop because of a circumstance or situation.

Let the customer know in a kind way that you understand the mistreatment they perhaps feel. Apologize to the customer and see if the two of you can meet half way to resolve the problem. I believe that there is always a way to demonstrate excellent customer service after all… God is a God of Excellence.

Customer service is an enormous 'pet peeve' of mine. I give excellent service and expect it back in return. If a person gives me fantastic service, I will go to the ends of the earth to make sure their supervisor knows and will do the same if I received terrible customer service.

Moreover, I will also let people know that the business which I patronize is excellent, or not. It's all about treating people the way you want to be addressed. Okay, so, one of your employees is having a bad day. Yes, we all have odd days but the employee who is having a hard time should not take it out on the consumer.

Body language, tone, facial expressions all play an important role in customer service good and bad. Email, phone conversations, and text messages all have a sound of emotion. Have you ever received an email or text message from someone and after you read it you immediately thought the person who sent it was angry with you, only to find out that was not the case at all?

Don't put Dan on the customer service phone line if he is a non-English speaking person. Don't misunderstand me; I have no issues with other nationalities, but really?? Come on now, we have all experienced "The phone call" yes, when you call, and that call turns into a headache, and you have to ask for a supervisor, and you have to call back the next day and then it turns into a nightmare. Who hires these people? Oh! The management of the business because the owner is nowhere around, therefore, most of the time the owner does not have a clue what is going on with the administration.

Don't put Sally Sue front and center of your company to greet customers or even answer the phone if she does not have the grace to smile or say hello in a happy voice and it looks as if you have just interrupted her day! I will give you two scenarios that I am sure you have encountered at some point.

<u>Scenario one:</u>

You: Walking into a business.

Sally Sue: Sitting at her desk in a detached I don't care voice and posture.

You: Hesitate to say something because Sally Sue is so nonchalant, glances at you and does not get up from her chair but with hesitation, you tell Sally Sue what you need.

Sally Sue: Slowly gets up without a smile, grabs your items, rings them up, throws your things in a bag, hands the bag to you, turns around, walks away and sits back down. There is no thank you said, come again, have a good day, nada!

You: standing there as if you have just been stripped naked. Now, what do you do? In situations like that, here is what I would do. With a smile on my face, I ask the person are they having a bad day. Depending on their response determines what I will say and do next. *(Example)* At a grocery store, the cashier was slinging my groceries all over the counter area as she was putting the items in the bag.

    As I watched her, she had no smile nor conversation. I said to her with a smile, "you must be having a bad day?" She replied, in a monotone voice "I don't want to be here." My response to her was "Yes, It shows because you are throwing my groceries all over the place. She then replied with an expression of embarrassment "oh I am sorry I didn't know it showed." I then replied, "Yes, it does, and the next customer may not be as nice as I." She stated," I'm sorry, thank you very much."

"Whatever a person is feeling within their self will most likely show up openly and even unaware."
– Dr. Christine Rice Slocumb

Now with that said, I did not contact her supervisor. The employee was made aware of her behavior and perhaps treated the next customer with excellent service.

Scenario two:

You: calling a company, the phone is ringing.

Dan: a non-English speaking person picks up the phone. Hello, how can I help you?

You: I would like to _____

Dan: Ah!" You say you would like to_____

You: Realizing agent can't understand nor speak English begin to speak slowly. No, I said I would like to _____

Dan: Okay, let me see what you say, you say you want to_____

You: after about the six responses of saying No, that is not what I said, become frustrated, because this call is now 30 minutes long. Then he puts you on hold. Seriously?

"Even though a person may not be from the same country the ability for gaining an understanding of words spoken is vital to excellent customer service."
– Dr. Christine Rice Slocumb

"Clear communication is a primary tool to success." – Dr. Christine Rice Slocumb

Did you know when speaking to someone over the phone you can sense if a person is smiling or not? Efficient customer service means helping people in a friendly manner. Here's a nugget for you. Sometimes even the customer may be having a bad day.
Say Whaaaat???

"Employee + Bad Day+ Customer's bad day = Disaster for business." – Dr. Christine Rice Slocumb

To set your business apart, always provide excellent customer service and mean it from your heart because most people can spot a fake and will not come back even if your product is worth it. However, most people will pay the extra cost or drive the extra miles for genuine service.

The new customer often receives special treatment; please don't forget to reward your long-term consumers with discounts, gifts, etc. Come up with creative ways to let them know you appreciate their business.

"It does not matter how many customers you have in your business, count them all individually special." – Dr. Christine Rice Slocumb

Most often people think if you are a Christian that Jesus images and scriptures have to be posted everywhere for the physical eye to see. There's nothing wrong with that, but here is something to remember. Everything starts from the inside then outwardly. Meaning, if you have love inside of you, it will reflect upon whomever you come in contact with, and they will see Christ demonstrated through you. Showing love is advantageous which cost you nothing.

Make sure your customer service demonstrates: **Empathy and compassion:** Put yourself in the customer shoes. If you were the consumer what would you want? Everybody is different with likes and dislikes. Therefore, you have to be mindful of the individuals you serve.

Respect, Joyfulness, and Insight: Give respect to your clients, and they will respect you. Be joyful in serving them and have the insight to know what they need. For instance, make sure everyone within your organization knows everything about the products and or services offered. **Knowledge is powerful,** without it, questions can't adequately be answered, and problems can't be solved to meet the consumers need.

Build Relationships with Repeated Consumers: Go the extra mile, understand what they need, then make sure they receive it every time.

Integrity and Diligence: Better is the poor who walks in his integrity than one perverse in his ways, though he be rich. (Proverbs 28:6)

If you find you cannot honor a deadline for whatever reason, contact your customer before the deadline and say so. Do not wait for the customer to confront you about being late.

If you notice an item in the customer's hand is damaged and the customer doesn't see it, bring it to their attention; don't let them pay full price or better yet, exchange it if you can or give them credit. Being honest in your dealings will take your company a long way. Attentiveness is the one customer service skill companies seem to overlook a bit. Paying close attention to detail in every area is vitally important; often it's in the small thing that makes the significant impact. Being attentive means keeping promises, and maintaining standards, being alert, making sure everything is decent and in order.

Can you remember when the internet began to hit mainstream society? It was such a captivating thing seeing and understanding the logic of communicating with someone from afar, but yet so close.

It was at that moment in time I saw then, the good, bad and the ugly side of what social media could become. As I was viewing, I wrote this poem titled

"Online Junkies" that went like this:

Online junkies get a natural high,

scanning the internet

A mind-blowing surprise.

Some are looking for a love mate,

With or without a face.

Along with a name that may be fake.

Online Junkies, what's on your mind?

Go ahead, say the word,

Type a few lines.

Searching for knowledge?

Informative information?

Download some files,

Just sit and be patient.

Newcomers watch out!

You just might get hooked.

All it takes is to sign on.

And take a look.

Then before you know it,

You're flying high.

The web caught you,

Now you're addicted for life.

    Let me remind you; I wrote that poem in the early stages of social media. I saw then, what is happening now. Social media and modern technology have taken a front seat across the entire nation. Corporations now have to be tech-savvy to be competitive. Depending on the usage, the internet can be beneficial or not. "You are hired" Nowadays upon hearing those words, come with a laptop and phone for mobility. Personal contact for filling out resumes and face to face interviews are the thing of the past. Now interviews and applications must be completed online.

Most corporations hire contract employees to save money; that can serve as a satellite office from home. It cuts down company overhead by doing it that way. And I get it! I truly understand. The economy for some is horrible right now. Hence what happens to the older generation who have not been trained to understand technology? They are scared to death, especially if they are 'grandfathered' in, sort of speak. With the marketplace implementing changes using a different technique, it can become overwhelming. Now you have tech stress within the workplace.

Moreover, you as the employer will have to provide training for those within your organization, and with the expectation, they are capable of grasping the concept and have the willingness to change.

When faced with change and the internal struggle to accept it, most people do not like it. Employers will need to encourage people to get on board and become a part of a new generation. Leaders will have to learn how to embrace change efficiently. You will also have to equip the new hires. Think long and hard about growing your business with Christ in the center and how your employees will be happy to come to work.

I remember when I was a Bereavement coordinator for Hospice, I loved going to work; arriving early two hours was my thing. It gave me a chance to meet the families who had to leave their loved ones and go to work. It allowed me to be there during a shift change to encourage my co-workers.

Did I have to do it? No, not at all. I did it because for me it was not a job but ministry. I did it because the establishment recognized Jesus. Therefore, the atmosphere was very inviting. I did it because it made a difference in the lives of those we served, as well as my co-workers.

In your business if you played soft inspirational music, you would be amazed by the inviting atmosphere, the energy level, and productivity that would instantly begin to flourish within your company. Employees will be happy to come to work and not in such a rush to leave.

"Who really does the work? And how do you the employer engage with the employees you hire? Find someone that has a passion for their job, and the work that they do, then equip them to do it, and you will have a trusted, happy, productive employee for life."
– Dr. Christine Rice Slocumb

CHAPTER 7

In establishing and growing your business, keep these simple tidbits in mind. God is concerned about the marketplace, and if you are a business owner, you should be concern about what Father God thinks about your business. Jesus cares about the public arena and everything involved; from trade centers, law, government, industry, and education.

He places His people in the workplace. In the Bible, the marketplace was the public square; that is where people handled all their business.

1. Develop an onsite or offsite grief support program for your employees. Most employers don't realize that grief is more than the death of a loved one. Often employees arrived to work already stressed and loaded down with issues. Having a safe place for employees to share and get help can be very beneficial for both parties.

To establish a support program inbox drchristinericeslocumb@gmail.com. I will be more than happy to set it up within your company and or be the contract advisor.

2. *"When you let God speak through your business, he will draw people to you, and your company will flourish because He is the head of your business."* - Dr. Christine Rice Slocumb

3. Treat others the same way you want them to treat you. (Luke 6:31 nasv)

4. *"A thriving business happens one client relationship at a time."* - Dr. Christine Rice Slocumb

5. *"You cannot grow a business apart from the support and encouragement of others."* - Dr. Christine Rice Slocumb

6. *"Happy employees produce grateful client relationships that last."* Dr. Christine Rice Slocumb

7. *"Since we are the vessels in the earth and God uses people, places and things to get the job done; appreciate everyone who may be a part of the team no matter what position they hold."*

8. *Healthy growth is a Godly process that will last forever.* - Dr. Christine Rice Slocumb

9. *"Sharing ideas and ways to help each other grow leads to improving and expanding a Kingdom –* Dr. Christine Rice Slocumb

10. *"A business that prays together is a great way to create a long-term investment and a lifetime of relationships with repeat customers." Dr. Christine Rice Slocumb"*

With today's economic downsizing, layoffs, mergers, and businesses are closing; millions are losing their jobs. Those that don't lose their jobs are having the task of carrying the extra load.
Every position level within a business in today's economy is on shaky ground. 401k, as well as health benefits, are not promising.

You as a business proprietor have the opportunity to impart greatness in the life of another person. You have the chance to show what it means to lead by example and with integrity in the marketplace. Equality within the workplace, for the most part, does not exist. You can make a difference internationally.

What would it look for you to have a multi-cultured organization, no prejudice? Could you do it? What would it look like for you to grow your business with Christ in the center?

"Trusting in God's provision for your business as well as your life is a sure win. As the dust settles after the economy plunders, the only thing that is going to stand or even matter is Jesus Christ the Lord and Savior of us all." – Dr. Christine Rice Slocumb

RESOURCES

Your word is a lamp to my feet and a light to my path. (Psalm 119: 105)

Psalm 5	Prayer for Guidance
Jeremiah 29:11.	God's plan towards you
Proverbs 16:3	Commitment
Proverbs 16: 11-13.	Honesty
Matthew 18: 21-35	Forgiveness
Mark 12:31	Love your neighbor
Romans 10:6-10	Righteousness of faith

Romans 8:28	All things work together
1st Samuel 16:7	Prejudice and Discrimination
Luke 6:38.	The law of Divine Reciprocity (Giving)
Jeremiah 17:7-8.	God's Provision
Deuteronomy 8:18	God gives the ability to produce Wealth

Other books by Dr. Christine Rice Slocumb

Artmu♪therapy
Shares a proven program that works to help people overcome grief, bereavement, and loss, along with any other obstacles or challenges. It guides them to experience victory in every area of their life.

Keeping It Real When Infidelity Strikes
It offers hope and inspiration to anyone who has experienced the heartbreak of infidelity -- whether in marriage or any intimate relationship. It's not just about an unfaith spouse but teaches you how to find and love yourself.

I'll Fly Away. Funeral Inspirations
With social media so easy to access and to take a front center stage, we as human beings have become so far removed from the personal touch of helping others. This book is inspirational, inspiring and encouraging for anyone who has had a loved one die. Every hospital, funeral home, civic organization, religious institution and the church should have one within their reach. To live is to die, to die is to live...

Words That Speak
Songs, Quotes, Poems and Short Stories. What's in a word? Do you know? Take a look, how deep will you go? Words, what do they mean? Words inspire, Set the soul on fire. Make you laugh, cry, smile, and can fill the heart's desire. But what matters most, is that Words speak.

Grieve Gods Way
Grieve God's Way is designed to help pastors, lay ministers, hospitals, doctors office, and other corporate organizations to set up a bereavement department or programs within their local church or business to effectively help those who grieve.

All books can be purchased through Amazon or other affiliations in the US and International.

Faith-Based Business

The partial listing below of faith businesses is a compliment of Trumpet Call to the Nations. http://www.trumpetcall2nations.com/faith-based-christian-businesses. This website shares a wealth of information. Their ministry is extraordinary. Thank you so much Trumpet Call Facilitators for being a blessing for the Kingdom of God.

Bethany Press International
http://www.bethanypress.com/
Partner of Bethany International, a fellowship of believers in Jesus Christ with a commitment to reach the world with His message by witnessing, training and sending missionaries, planting churches, and printing Christian literature. Revenue generated by Bethany Press provides support for the ministries of Bethany International.

Bluefish TV   https://www.bluefishtv.com/
Non-profit Christian video publishing company based in Richardson, Texas. Bluefish TV works with well-known Christian speakers and authors to produce small group studies and video illustrations that help people teach in their church.

Curves   https://www.curves.com/
Founder Gary Heavin Christian values permeate the woman's health club company

Prince of Peace® Enterprises, Inc.
http://popus.com/

Founder is a man faithful to God's leadership. Through his choice of our company name, one can tell that our philosophy is built upon the ethical principles of the evangelical Christian faith. Kenneth Yeung attributes his successes to God's guidance and blessings. Our top sellers include Tiger Balm®, Prince of Peace® Ginseng & Teas, Bee & Flower Soap, Han's Honey Loquat, and more. These lines can be found in all the major health food chains. Many high quality European and American products such as Delacre® assorted cookies, Ferrero Rocher® chocolates, Almond Roca®, Loacker® Wafer and Ricola® Natural Cough Drops are among the exclusively distributed line.

Car battery giant Interstate Batteries http://www.interstatebatteries.com/ has a "self-avowed religious identity and is very open in their God talk" in internal training and communication.

Retail giant Wal-Mart http://www.walmart.com/ has used Christian servant leadership models in building the world's largest retailer.

Former heavyweight boxer George Foreman became an ordained minister after a religious experience in 1977 and continues to share his religious experiences in the media and on Christian television today. George Foreman Cooking http://www.georgeforemancooking.com/ has grown from the George Foreman Grill into other products, including cookbooks, home and car cleaning products, vitamins and supplements, and personal care products.

United States Plastic Corporation
http://www.usplastic.com/

Founder, Dr. R. Stanley Tam, made a promise to God that if God prospered this business, he would honor God in any way he could. God has consistently done His part and, with His help, we do ours to the best of our ability. Mr. Tam has placed 100% of the ownership of United States Plastic Corp. into a foundation whose purpose is to establish churches in third world countries.

Business as Mission Resources

Mission-To release the power of business to transform people, communities, and nations for the glory of God.

Cards from Africa-Rwanda
http://cardsfromafrica.com/

Cards from Africa is a part of a new generation of African businesses making high-quality products, in one of the poorest countries, available to the international market at competitive prices. The business model is to provide a stepping-stone for staff to transition easily to another career or start their own business someday.

Olive Technology   http://olivetechnology.com/

Core values- Values such as integrity, honesty and the pursuit of professional excellence are a reflection of an individual's self-image, created by their religious beliefs, their family experience, and life lessons.

We have found that people with similar values work well together, work harder, teach each other, hold each other accountable and deliver a work product that serves the client well.

C12 Group   http://www.c12group.com/

C12 is a fee-for-service for-profit organization that operates on membership dues. Prospective members must be invited to join. C12 is a blend of Christian business leadership best practices and general management tools coupled with Godly counsel, accountability, Christian business coaching, a focus on spiritual values and needs, and practical ways to run businesses based on Biblical principles for the eternal benefit of stakeholders.

Convene http://www.convenenow.com/

Membership organization to connect, equip, and inspire Christian CEOs and Business Owners to grow exceptional businesses, become higher-impact leaders and honor God.

EC Group India   http://ecgroup-intl.com/

In 1999, Tom Sudyk, CEO, and founder of EC Group International established e-commerce operations in Chennai, India. The vision for expanding to India served two purposes. One purpose was to provide small and medium-sized US companies' safe access to the abundant talent India had to offer. The second purpose was to establish a company that would make a difference to the people it touched.

House Blend Café-Eat Good Do Good http://houseblendcafe.com/

The concept of House Blend Cafe developed over the course of several years of dreaming of a creative way to connect with people and impact lives - 100% of net profits are used to love and serve people in the local community and around the world (feeding the homeless, funding services for women and children in need, home renovation projects and helping to restore neighborhoods, supporting other people who have a heart to serve, and starting other House Blend Café's in other communities).

Right now ministries-Work as Worship Network
http://www.workasworshipnetwork.org/

Mission to help people see their work differently. Work is an opportunity to worship the God who created us.

Redemptive Business Consulting
http://www.redemptivebusinessconsulting.com/

Redemptive Business Consultants exist to leverage business to eliminate spiritual and physical poverty in the world. Through business analysis and customized training, Redemptive Business Consultants is committed to redeeming business to better impact the world.

Pacific Resources International-China
http://www.priusa.com/

PRI is an organization with expertise in building businesses in China and surrounding regions. PRI is headed up by a team comprised of individuals from the United States, New Zealand, South Africa, and Malaysia, and is focused on building best practice business operations.

Meixia International China   http://integrated-life.org/meixia-international/

Bill Job, an American who moved to Xiamen, China in 1987 to study Chinese ended up starting Meixia, a company that produces exceptional stained glass products which is also his ministry.

Partners Worldwide http://www.partnersworldwide.org/
Partner with local business champions and networks that care about their communities know the business environment and can build on the local resources. Engage and support network of businesspeople through global partnerships and personal relationships.

Delta Jewels   http://www.deltajewels.com/
Girl power fuels beautiful jewelry
Delta Jewels is a youth development initiative that empowers young women to realize their potential, inspires creativity and encourages community through jewelry design. All jewelry is designed and handmade by these young women and profits go directly to the designer of each piece.

Selam Awassa   http://www.selamawassa.org/
Advancing agriculture in Africa
Selam Awassa Business Group focuses on the design and production of appropriate technology for the rural community. With the help of the research and development organization of the Ethiopian government, SABG stays abreast of developments in the technology sector. Beyond renewable energy

products, SABG produces equipment for smallholder farmers and the construction industry.

All's Fair World Gifts
http://www.allsfairworldgifts.com/

Gifts you can feel good about giving All's Fair brings fair-trade coffee, tea, nativities, crosses, collectibles, clothes and other items to San Antonio, Texas, from all over the world. Fairtrade means no slave labor or sweatshops, and no environmentally unfriendly practices. All's Fair is committed to making San Antonio — and the world — a better place.

The Source Café-Uganda
http://www.kibogroup.org/

One of the best known and most reputable cafes in Jinja is the Source Cafe Katie Davis also has an office nearby for Amazima Ministries

Water Missions International
http://www.watermissions.org/

Water Missions International is a nonprofit Christian engineering organization providing sustainable, safe water and sanitation solutions for people in developing countries and disaster areas.

Missions Organizations and Networks
Includes a selection of established agencies with a business as mission focus or entity, plus specialist business as mission and 'tentmaker' agencies.

The Lausanne Movement
http://www.lausanne.org/en/

A global movement that mobilizes evangelical leaders to collaborate for world evangelization.

World Evangelical Alliance
http://www.worldea.org/
A global ministry working with local churches around the world to join in common concern to live and proclaim the Good News of Jesus in their communities.

Food for the Hungry https://fh.org/
Responding to God's call to end physical and spiritual hungers worldwide since 1971.

U.S. Center for World Mission
https://www.uscwm.org/
Mission- To catalyze believers to engage in developing communities of faith in Jesus Christ within the remaining unreached peoples on earth.

Christian Missionary Fellowship International
http://www.cmfi.org/
CMF Marketplace Ministries arm helps mobilize business professionals to the world's marketplaces where there is no witness.

Church Missionary Society   http://www.cms-uk.org/
CMS supports business as mission as a strategy and CMS Africa facilitates the BAM Africa network.

Frontiers   https://www.frontiersusa.org/
Frontiers has been pioneering for-profit business strategies to share the love of Christ in the Muslim world.

Global Disciples Network
http://globaldisciples.org/
The Global Access track has the specific aim to mobilize church planters through business.

Global Opportunities   http://www.globalopps.org/
Empowering tentmakers to reach the world. GO has free resources and training available on its site, plus tent making stories, news and events.

Interserve   http://www.interserve.org/
Interserve has pioneered in the area of business as mission, placing professionals and starting enterprises in the Arab World and Asia.

OMF International   http://omf.org/
Missional business, reaching people for Christ through businesses centered in a mission purpose, is a developing strategy of OMF International.

Operation Mobilization   http://www.omusa.org/
Supporting business people to bring about spiritual, social, economic and environmental transformation, using their skills in the heart of a community.

Pioneers http://www.pioneers.org/
Pioneers emphasizes non-traditional missionary methods, including business strategies, to meet spiritual and practical needs in communities.

SIM (Serving in Mission)   http://www.sim.org/
SIM helps those with business and professional skills get involved in mission through their business ministry opportunities.

Creative Development Ministries LTD
http://www.creativemin.org/
Uses the proceeds of a business as a way of financing mission.

The Crossover Foundation
http://foundation.crossoverusa.org/
Uses planned giving instruments such as wills, living trusts, annuities, and gifts in kind, and other financial arrangements to fund its church planting efforts.

Crossover Communications International (CCI)
http://crossoverusa.org/
An international church planting movement, intensely desires to see God glorified among all the peoples of the world. Founded in 1987, today CCI serves on all six continents and has planted many churches among the least reached peoples of the world.

World Horizons   http://www.worldhorizons.org/
Enables pioneering and creative mission, including an emphasis on business as mission.

World Venture / Transformational Ventures
http://tventures.worldventure.com/
World Venture has a business as mission arm called Transformational Ventures which has a focus on connecting business people with opportunities to serve.

YWAM (Youth With A Mission)
http://www.ywam.org/
YWAM has embraced business as mission as an avenue for missionary service. In addition, our

Business as Mission Resource Centre seeks to serve the broader movement by providing resources and training.

A Child's Hope Fund
http://www.achildshopefund.org/
Helps fight pediatric cancer, diabetes and hunger through medical and food programs, health education and emotional/spiritual support for children in nine countries endangered by disease, poverty, war and natural disaster.

AAA Charity Investment Fund
http://www.aaacharityinvestmentfund.org/
Outreach of World-Wide Missions seeking to assist donors in making wise and productive choices in their charitable giving. With over 60 years of experience and numerous projects options available, AAACIF's intention is to link donors with opportunities to "invest" in programs and causes that bring positive change to human lives. AAA Charity Investment Fund was formerly known as Emergency Relief Response Fund.

Business Funding/Micro Enterprise Organizations
Organizations that focus on business incubation- many provide mentoring, training and funds to develop businesses.

BPN Foundation-USA
http://www.bpn.ch/index.php?id=3&L=1
A private, nonprofit organization whose purpose is to connect business men and women of the western world with entrepreneurs of the developing world in

order to help these entrepreneurs create and build sustaining businesses that will enable them to improve the standard of living in their communities, fund the work of their local churches, and raise the social impact of Christians in their country.

Faith Partners   http://www.faithpartners.asia/
Social enterprise incubator started in Indonesia and dedicated to help communities overcome poverty through establishing self-sustaining small and medium businesses leading to positive social changes.

Integra   http://www.integrausa.org/
Provides training and loans for aspiring entrepreneurs in Central and Eastern Europe and Russia. Integra seeks to instill a 'business as mission' philosophy in their SME clients, helping them see their business as transformational.

Kingdom Venture Partners
http://www.kingdomventures.com/
A venture capital firm that invests in kingdom companies.

Hope International
http://www.hopeinternational.org/
Shares the hope of Christ as they provide biblically based training, savings services, and loans that restore dignity and break the cycle of poverty.

Non Profit Business Funding
Kiva   http://www.kiva.org/
A non-profit organization with a mission to connect people through lending to alleviate poverty.

Leveraging the internet and a worldwide network of microfinance institutions, Kiva lets individuals lend as little as $25 to help create opportunity around the world.

Global Hand   http://www.globalhand.org/en
Redistributes gifts in kind and donates inventory to business startups that are focused on creating jobs for the poor.

Trade as One   http://tradeasone.com/
Focused on creating a sustainable route to market for sustainable businesses that break cycles of poverty and dependency in the developing world.

Corporate World Meets Jesus

www.ingramcontent.com/pod-product-compliance
Lightning Source LLC
Chambersburg PA
CBHW040224220526
45473CB00001B/115